SIMPLE HARMONY

Thoughts on Holistic Christian Life

LARRY DUGGINS

COLUMKILLE
— PRESS —

FOREWORD

I am grateful to many people who have helped me to think through the model and everything that sits behind it:

The pastors and staff of White's Chapel UMC

My friend and mentor Dr. Elaine Heath

My seminary friends who have been and continue to be my community – Blair, Vance, Shellie, Amy, Mary Beth, Brittany, Autumn and many, many others

The 2011-12 class of the Academy for Missional Wisdom who worked through an early draft of this book and made many wise observations

And especially my family – Jay, Katie, Travis, Chris, and now Alex.

I am blessed by you all!

LARRY DUGGINS

Southlake, TX

2012

INTRODUCTION

We were sitting in the airport in Dallas, waiting to board the plane for our inaugural Perkins School of Theology international immersion class in Celtic Christian spiritual traditions. The group buzzed with excitement as we chatted about going to the ancient monastic sites of Iona and Lindesfarne, and the new monastic Northumbria Community. The trip would be a pilgrimage, I reminded them. Journaling, a daily office, and other formational experiences would be at the center of our journey together. Upon our return to the U.S. they would write academic papers in which they would reflect upon some aspect of Celtic spirituality that could enliven contemporary practices of worship or evangelism in their own churches.

Looking around at the dozen or so students, I recognized all but one, a 50-something, white-haired man whose theological education, I surmised, was probably not in readiness for his first career. I introduced myself, asking what he hoped to do upon graduation. Larry said he wanted to develop young adult ministries in non-traditional spaces, especially to provide community, mission, and worship opportunities for people who don't fit well in established churches.

Having just written two books on emerging and new monastic forms of ministry, and having[1] begun two experimental new monastic, missional communities just a year earlier,[2] I snapped to attention. We talked on, our voices growing increasingly animated as we shared ideas, dreams, and current situations. Little did we know that this conversation would spark the beginning of a shared pilgrimage that would go far beyond that initial journey to Iona.

Over the next few days while we worshipped, lived, and learned in the "thin space" of Celtic monastic communities, God clarified Larry's call to the work of what has now become the Missional Wisdom Foundation. Once a brilliant entrepreneur in the world of finance and business, Larry is now an Elder in the United Methodist Church and has become a beloved mentor to many who are learning to serve in missional, spiritually disciplined leadership roles in the church. Today Larry is the director of the Missional Wisdom Foundation and co-director of the Epworth Project, a network of new monastic houses in the Dallas-Ft. Worth metroplex. He also teaches in the Academy for Missional Wisdom, a training program that equips people to start and lead missional micro-communities. The fruitfulness of Larry's life is a result of his own practice of what he thinks of as "simple harmony."

Simple Harmony is the first of what I expect will be many books written by my friend and colleague, Larry Duggins. This little volume captures so beautifully the ancient rhythms of "filling up and pouring out," or the balance

---

1 *The Mystic Way of Evangelism: A Contemplative Vision for Christian Outreach* (Grand Rapids: Baker Academic, 2008), and *Longing for Spring: A New Vision for Wesleyan Community,* (Eugene: Cascade, 2010).

2 New Day and The Epworth Project, www.peopleofnewday.com and www.missionalwisdom.com

between contemplation and action. Using the Celtic cross as a visual aid, Larry describes the four quadrants of the balanced life, and the unity of a life lived in harmony with the triune God. The way of life described in this book is one that is deeply evangelistic, for it is a life lived immersed in the Holy Spirit, filled with love of God and neighbor. I have seen Larry teach the principles in this book to groups of clergy and lay people, and have watched them awaken and grow because of the wisdom contained in these pages.

I thank God for Larry and for this book of spiritual theology, *Simple Harmony*. May this slender volume bring insight, renewal, and conviction to all of us who read it. May the simplicity of a life lived in harmony with the Jesus of the Gospels become through us a beacon of hope and welcome to our neighbors.

REV. ELAINE A. HEATH, PH.D.

April 16, 2012

Southern Methodist University

Dallas, Texas

ONE

I am Confused

The number of Torah commandments that are obligatory for all generations is 613: 248 of them are positive commandments, whose mnemonic is the number of parts in the human body; 365 of them are negative commandments, whose mnemonic is the number of days in the solar year.

MAIMONIDES IN THE MISHNEH TORAH
AS TRANSLATED BY MECHON MAMRE

Tradition holds that Maimonides, the famous Jewish rabbi, philosopher, and mystic of 12th century Spain, compiled the authoritative list of the 613 mitzvoth or commandments of the Torah. Maimonides searched the Scriptures and documented the rules – both the things an observant Jewish person should and should not do in daily life. His efforts reflect an ongoing challenge for Jews and Christians: How does one embrace the Law and the Prophets in such a way that allows them to be fully incorporated into daily life? Are there truly 613 rules that we must remember to please God, and if so, how in the world can we remember them as we live our lives? Are there even more rules to live by when Christian people take the teachings of the New Testament into account?

It is my belief that Jesus dramatically simplified our task of compliance with the law through his life and his teachings. Jesus frequently argued with the religious scholars of his day for dwelling on the letter of the law and missing its intent. He criticized leaders who emphasized compliance with the tiny details of the law while ignoring the overarching theme of God's love.

The four Gospels are full of examples of Jesus being condemned by religious people for healing people on the Sabbath. It is easy to dismiss those leaders as hypocrites, but I am sure that many of them honestly believed that the Sabbath rules, which were part of those 613 commandments that Maimonides later documented, were to be literally upheld in all circumstances. In modern life, lots of people view Christianity in this way. They either struggle to identify and live under strict rules that they find in the Bible, or they reject Christianity altogether because they are unwilling to live under a set of rules that they don't really accept or understand. Exclusively focusing on the rules divides people into groups of those who follow and those who do not, and makes it both simple and natural to live life by judging others through our own personal understanding of the rules. I just don't think that is what Jesus had in mind.

The problem is that many folks use the "rules" to define their understanding of what a Christian person is to do in everyday life. Theologians talk about this issue as the question of human "vocation." Many people associate the word "vocation" with work, with what we do to earn a living. In this book, I would like to expand our understanding of vocation beyond simply what we do to earn money to a much broader definition that includes what we do in life. Seen this way, vocation is an answer to the oldest of questions: "Why do we exist?"

It seems unlikely that many of us would be comfortable taking a job without understanding what was expected of us in that job. We would want to know our working hours, what tasks would be expected of us, what tools would be available, and what we would be paid. We would spend time and energy before we accepted a job to develop a good understanding of what would be expected of us and what we could expect to receive in return.

Yet, many of us have no idea what a Christian person is to spend their time doing! When asked, most people will say something vague about being good or about loving people, but they cannot put their "job description" precisely into words. The issue becomes even cloudier when folks try to explain precisely how they should go about Christian life, or even why they should live in a certain way. It is no wonder that so many contemporary people have trouble relating to Christianity when Christian people have problems describing what Christian life is all about.

Thankfully, there are Scriptures that address Jesus' teachings on the task of humanity, his approach to acting in the world, and his statement of the goal of his ministry. We can look at those Scriptures together to create a simple matrix that illuminates the tasks and spirit of a balanced and healthy Christian life, a life of simple harmony. These Scriptures shed light on the balance of doing and being that Christ calls us to embrace. They help us to understand what a Christian person is to focus on in daily life, how we are to do those things, and why we are to do them. Scripture helps us to understand the human vocation – why we are here in the first place.

Food For Thought

Does Christianity ever feel like a set of rules that you must follow? Could you see where society might feel that?

What do you think a balanced and healthy life as a Christian looks like?

Do Jesus' teachings help you understand that view?

TWO

The Greatest Commandment

When the Pharisees heard that he had silenced the Sadducees, they gathered together, and one of them, a lawyer, asked him a question to test him. "Teacher, which commandment in the law is the greatest?" He said to him, " 'You shall love the Lord your God with all your heart, and with all your soul, and with all your mind.' This is the greatest and first commandment. And a second is like it: 'You shall love your neighbor as yourself.' On these two commandments hang all the law and the prophets."

MATTHEW 22:34-40

The first of the three anchor passages is often referred to as "The Greatest Commandment." In the passage, Jesus is involved in an extended conversation with a group of priests, Pharisees and Sadducees, who have confronted him regarding his authority. Earlier in the day, as reported in Matthew 21, Jesus had entered the Temple and driven out the vendors and had overturned the money-changing tables. The Temple's figures of authority confronted Jesus, questioning him about his behavior and about his authority to act as he did. The exchange takes place during the climactic week of Jesus' ministry that culminated with the death and resurrection.

Matthew 22:23 identifies the people who questioned Jesus as the Chief Priests and elders of the people. Later in the chapter, we learn that those elders included Pharisees and Sadducees, who were members of religious factions that interpreted the Torah differently. According to the *New Interpreter's Dictionary of the Bible* (Abingdon Press, 2009), the Pharisees were more aligned with the common people and thought of themselves as upholding the traditions of Moses, while the Sadducees tended to be more aristocratic and were more closely tied to the priestly traditions. It was quite common for the two groups to debate interpretation with one another, and it would have been expected that elders of both traditions would participate in the Temple leadership.

The Temple's figures of authority challenged Jesus with a direct question regarding his authority, but Jesus invoked his status as a rabbi to answer their question with a question. When the Temple authorities could not answer Jesus' query to them, Jesus then invoked his right not to answer them directly. Instead, he takes the opportunity to teach three parables that describe the ministry of John the Baptist, the ministry of Jesus, and the coming of the kingdom of God, all of which reflected poorly on the Temple authorities.

The Pharisees and Sadducees then asked Jesus a series of questions that seem to be intended to entrap Jesus in an anti-government or blasphemous position so that his words might be used against him. The resulting questions and answers include important teachings on taxation, resurrection, and the identity of the Messiah, and they also include Jesus' pivotal statement on the nature of the vocation of humanity - to love God with all the heart, soul, and mind, and to love others as oneself.

The response of Jesus was grounded in the Torah. His response begins with the first of the Ten Commandments as related in Deuteronomy 6:5. The commandment to love God completely with one's entire being was especially familiar to the Pharisees, who included this passage in the phylacteries worn on their bodies. A phylactery is a set of pouches with straps that would be filled with Scripture and then strapped to the forehead and arms. The commandment to love others is found in Leviticus 19:18 in the midst of a teaching on just and moral behavior. Jesus the rabbi places the two commandments in relationship with one another in a way that allows them to amplify one another.

In the Greatest Commandment as it is presented in Matthew, Jesus Christ presents a very clear statement detailing precisely how people are to order their lives and spend their time. By their very definition, commandments are directives - not suggestions, not options, not possibilities - but imperative statements of that which is to be done. Jesus begins by giving God priority and by saying that we are to love God with our entire being, using all the gifts of our heart, mind, and soul. He then equates a second commandment to the first, instructing us to love our neighbor as we love ourselves. Jesus concludes his response with a remarkable statement that sharpens our reaction - he concludes that all of the law and the prophets are based on these two commands - that this is what we are to focus on in the world.

The Greatest Commandment becomes an even more powerful statement in the context of Matthew 23, which immediately follows it. In that chapter, Jesus levels a series of scathing accusations against the scribes and Pharisees in some of the strongest language attributed to him in the Gospels. Jesus condemns the practice of emphasizing form over substance – of focusing on rule-keeping rather than justice. He accuses the leaders of completely missing the point of God's teachings by focusing on compliance to minutia and caring about outward appearances rather than dedicating themselves to love. When read in sequence, it seems very clear that Jesus says that loving God and loving others is the most important duty a person can have, and that to emphasize anything else leads to woe.

Variations on the Greatest Commandment appear in all four Gospels. In the variation found in Mark 12:28-34, the context remains an inquiry into the authority of Jesus by the Temple hierarchy, but with some interesting differences. In Mark, the questioner is a scribe, not a Pharisee, and Mark describes the motivation for the question as true curiosity driven by a respect for Jesus' responses to the questions of others. The scribe affirms the response of Jesus by quoting supporting Scripture, and Jesus responds favorably to the wisdom of the scribe by commenting that "You are not far from the kingdom of God" in v. 34. The less adversarial exchange between Jesus and the scribe allows space for Jesus to associate the love of God and neighbor with the coming of the kingdom.

In the variation included in Luke 10:25-37, the statement occurs much earlier in the ministry of Jesus and is associated with the parable of the Good Samaritan. The questioner is identified as a "lawyer" - likely a scribe - in the NRSV, and his motivation is to test Jesus. The question is different in this version - the lawyer asks what must be done to achieve eternal life and Jesus responds by reflecting the question back to the lawyer for a response. The lawyer then responds citing the love of God and the love of neighbor, and Jesus affirms the correctness of his response. The lawyer then quibbles about the definition of neighbor, providing Jesus with an entree to teach about service to others in a countercultural manner that contrasts religiosity with compassion. Jesus establishes the Greatest Commandment as the path to eternal life and then challenges the assumption that the religious hierarchy is on that path.

In the Book of John, Jesus follows the foot washing of the disciples and the Last Supper with an extensive summary of his teaching, which has come to be known as the "Farewell Discourse." In this teaching, Jesus speaks of a "new commandment" twice, once in 13:34-35 and again in 15:12, emphasizing the importance of loving each other. Jesus commands the disciples to love each other as he has loved them, and identifies this love as the identifying mark of his disciples. In John, Jesus is not explicit about the love of God, but he links himself extensively to the Father, implicitly equating love of Jesus with love of God. In his commandment in 15:12, Jesus reiterates his instruction that the disciples' love for each other be modeled on his love for them.

Matthew 22:34-40	Mark 12:28-31	Luke 10:25-28	John 13:34-35
When the Pharisees heard that he had silenced the Sadducees, they gathered together, and one of them, a lawyer, asked him a question to test him. 'Teacher, which commandment in the law is the greatest?' He said to him, ' "You shall love the Lord your God with all your heart, and with all your soul, and with all your mind." This is the greatest and first commandment. And a second is like it: "You shall love your neighbor as yourself." On these two commandments hang all the law and the prophets.'	One of the scribes came near and heard them disputing with one another, and seeing that he answered them well, he asked him, 'Which commandment is the first of all?' Jesus answered, 'The first is, "Hear, O Israel: the Lord our God, the Lord is one; you shall love the Lord your God with all your heart, and with all your soul, and with all your mind, and with all your strength." The second is this, "You shall love your neighbor as yourself." There is no other commandment greater than these.'	Just then a lawyer stood up to test Jesus. 'Teacher,' he said, 'what must I do to inherit eternal life?' He said to him, 'What is written in the law? What do you read there?' He answered, 'You shall love the Lord your God with all your heart, and with all your soul, and with all your strength, and with all your mind; and your neighbor as yourself.' And he said to him, 'You have given the right answer; do this, and you will live.'	I give you a new commandment, that you love one another. Just as I have loved you, you also should love one another. By this everyone will know that you are my disciples, if you have love for one another.'

The commandment to love one another also appears as a central teaching throughout the epistles, appearing explicitly in Romans 13:8-10, Galatians 5:14, 1 John 3:23 and James 2:8. The theme recurs with sufficient frequency as to demand attention.

Jesus was asked to identify the most important commandment and his response identifies two – the passage from Matthew goes so far as to explicitly use sequencing language with Jesus placing the love of God as the first and greatest commandment, following with the love of neighbor by saying "a second is like it." It seems that Jesus sees the two commandments as intertwined with each other to the point that he is unwilling to present one without the other.

The various scriptural descriptions of the Greatest Commandment combine to identify it as the central teaching of the Law and Prophets, a mark of the kingdom of God, the path to eternal life, and the mark of disciples of Jesus Christ. It is a clear statement of Christian vocation – a mission for life – a clear direction of what a Christian person should spend time and energy doing.

Food For Thought

Using the description in the Gospels of what the Greatest Commandment is, how does this describe how we should live? What does this look like in your life?

What draws you away from living a life focused on loving God and loving others?

How do you define "others"? Do "others" include everyone other than yourself?

THREE

The Hymn of Kenosis

If then there is any encouragement in Christ, any consolation from love, any sharing in the Spirit, any compassion and sympathy, make my joy complete: be of the same mind, having the same love, being in full accord and of one mind. Do nothing from selfish ambition or conceit, but in humility regard others as better than yourselves. Let each of you look not to your own interests, but to the interests of others. Let the same mind be in you that was in Christ Jesus, who, though he was in the form of God,

did not regard equality with God as something to be exploited, but emptied himself

taking the form of a slave, being born in human likeness.

And being found in human form, he humbled himself

and became obedient to the point of death—

even death on a cross.

Therefore God also highly exalted him

and gave him the name that is above every name,

so that at the name of Jesus every knee should bend,

in heaven and on earth and under the earth,

and every tongue should confess

that Jesus Christ is Lord, to the glory of God the Father.

PHILIPPIANS 2:1-11

The second anchor Scripture is the "Hymn of Kenosis", a Greek word that means to "pour out." In this passage, Paul urges the people of the Church of Philippi to reject ambition and conceit and to look to the needs of others as Christ did. The passage includes a dense and rhythmic stanza describing Jesus "pouring himself out" for humanity, which may have relied on a traditional hymn about Jesus. The hymn described a figurative descent and ascent by

Jesus, who set aside his rightful status as the Son of God and emptied himself in service and obedience to the extreme of enduring a humiliating death, only to be exalted by God and raised to an eternal Lordship.

The passage teaches the listener to set aside even rightful entitlements in "emptying oneself" in service to God and to others. The passage implies a need for the listeners to be filled by their "encouragement in Christ," their "consolation in love," and their "sharing in the Spirit" so that the pouring out might take place. The Philippians are to be filled by their connection to Christ and community through the Spirit, and to be emptied in their pouring out in service.

If the mission of the church is to share God's love in the world, the ministry of the church is the action of implementing the mission. It may be possible to engage in some of the aspects of Christian life with an entirely self-centered perspective, but efforts to do so will ultimately fail or be transformed into an outwardly focused endeavor. The way that the ministry of the church is lived is the pouring out and filling up described within the "Hymn of Kenosis." Pouring out in Christian living is intuitively more identifiable with the traditional concepts of ministry. Preaching and teaching are examples of a pouring out in the love of God - actions of self-giving that empower others and that work toward the making of disciples. Similarly, feeding the poor, caring for the sick, visiting the prisoner, and freeing the oppressed are examples described in Matthew 25 as examples of pouring out in love of others. Ministry in these examples takes place on two levels - actually performing the acts and empowering others to do so.

The kenotic nature of performing the actions as an individual is practically self-evident. The actions involve a giving of time, energy, resources, gifts, and graces on the part of the individual to empower others to worship, to learn, or to have physical or emotional needs addressed. The actions involve a transfer of a benefit of some type, be it physical, spiritual, or emotional, from the actor to the recipient as a physical manifestation of the grace of God.

Empowering others to act kenotically – to pour themselves out – is a different gift. It is a recognition that in some cases, specialized training, education, or organizational skills might be needed in order to facilitate individual acts of kenosis. In these cases, the gift of the giver is not targeted directly to the recipient, but is rather a gift of empowerment to other Christians to allow them to pour out their gifts directly to participants. This idea of ministry is directly related to the Apostle Paul's descriptions of the body of Christ, in which the various members of the body bring their particular gifts and talents to bear in the service of Christ. The gifts of coordination and education allow the body of Christ to be more effective, matching needs and resources on a broader scale.

In order to "pour out" on a consistent basis, one must occasionally pause to "fill up." Logic dictates that one cannot pour out continuously without occasionally replenishing the supply. If the gifts poured out are spiritual, emotional, and physical, then attention must be given to periodically replenishing each of these resources.

Spiritual "filling up" takes place largely within the means of grace, including the practices of prayer, the Lord's Supper, reading Scripture, and worship. It is interesting to note that filling up involves both the pouring out of grace from God and the pouring out efforts of fellow members within the body of Christ, empowered by God. Seen in that light, worship includes both filling up and pouring out by various individuals. From that perspective, it is possible to view the acts of filling up as acts of ministry, because they enable a person to ultimately pour out themselves. One can then see acts of solitary prayer and individual self-care as integral components of ministry.

Filling up also comes through the acts of others in forms of being loved and accepting generosity, care, and forgiveness from others. Being a humble recipient requires setting aside the myth of self-sufficiency and the pride and hubris associated with it. The putting away of the old self that Paul describes in Ephesians 4 enables the concerns of the old self to be set aside in the filling up of the new self to enable pouring out in support of the mission of the church. In this way, the attributes of humility, receptiveness, and submission of self can be viewed as components of ministry.

If the Greatest Commandment is the answer to the *what* of Christian life, kenosis is the answer to *how* the love of God and the love of others is to be lived. We are to pour ourselves out in love and in service, and in order to do that, we must pause to be filled.

Food For Thought

Paul asks the Church of Philippi to reject ambition and conceit in order to look to the needs of others. What might be getting in your way of serving others? Does the world urge you to think this way?

In using the image of pouring out and filling up, what would you be pouring out and what would you want to fill up with?

At this time in your life, are you full or empty? Explain.

What are some examples of ways you refill?

FOUR

The Unity Prayer

I ask not only on behalf of these, but also on behalf of those who will believe in me through their word, that they may all be one. As you, Father, are in me and I am in you, may they also be in us, so that the world may believe that you have sent me. The glory that you have given me I have given them, so that they may be one, as we are one, I in them and you in me, that they may become completely one, so that the world may know that you have sent me and have loved them even as you have loved me.

JOHN 17:20-23

The final anchor passage is John 17: 20-23, which I refer to as the "Unity Prayer." It is a portion of Jesus' long prayer for the disciples and the world immediately prior to his betrayal. In John 13, Jesus joins his disciples for a meal on the evening before Passover. After washing their feet and sending Judas away, Jesus delivers an extensive teaching to the disciples, teaching that they should love one another, anticipate the coming of the Holy Spirit, and live firmly based in love of Jesus.

Upon the completion of his teaching, Jesus turns to God in prayer, asking that his disciples and those who will come to believe because of their word be brought into unity with each other and with Jesus and God. The prayer found in John 17 is sometimes referred to as the "High Priestly Prayer" because of Jesus' role as intercessor for his follow-ers. Jesus asks that believers everywhere enter into the same unity with Christ and God that Jesus and God enjoy with one another.

Jesus asks God to join his disciples and the disciples of future generations together as Jesus and God are joined. Jesus repeats his petition several times while emphasizing the connection between God and himself, the disciples and himself, and God and the disciples. Verses 22 and 23 highlight the role of Jesus as the mediator, passing the glory given him by God on to the disciples in order to create a connection between God and the disciples through the connection of Jesus to each of them. These verses give voice to the restorative role of Christ the Redeemer, who asks God to include us in their perfect loving relationship.

The idea of unity with God is called theosis and it is a concept that flows back to very early Christian tradition.

The idea is repeated in 2 Peter 1:4, which states that the work of Jesus Christ has made it possible for us to become "participants of the divine nature." The concept of theosis has been more actively incorporated into the theology of the Eastern Church, but it appears in the thought of Thomas Aquinas and Martin Luther. The idea is embodied in the ideas of entire sanctification and growing in holiness that were developed by John Wesley and are central to United Methodist theology. The concept is that through the power of the Holy Spirit and the surrender of the human will to God, people can grow closer and closer to God until the human will aligns with the will of God. This does not transform the human into God, but rather into a union with God and God's energies. That union helps us to more fully understand how God acts through humanity in the world.

The prayer of Jesus addresses the *why* of Christian life, the rationale behind the mission of Christ. All of the miracles and signs, all of the joys and trauma, the very life of Jesus himself, find voice in the prayer of Jesus. Jesus loves us so that we may share the love that the Trinity shares, with the persons of the Trinity and with each other. Jesus' first petition in the passage is a request that God grant his followers loving community among themselves, a oneness that echoes the loving community between Father and Son.

The three core Scriptures combine to address the *what, how* and *why* of Christian life. As with all meaningful explanations, the three Scriptures also interact with each other to help us with what it means to live them together.

Food For Thought

Why did you decide to be a Christian?

How does Jesus' prayer help define why Christians live a certain way?

Does it surprise you that Jesus does not mention heaven in his prayer?

FIVE

The Simple Harmony Model

Seen in relationship to each other, the Greatest Commandment represents the vocation of humanity, the Hymn of Kenosis represents the method by which the vocation is to be fulfilled, and the Unity Prayer represents the goal of that vocation. The three Scriptures can be represented graphically in the form of a Celtic cross, which illustrates their interconnectedness. The commands to love God and to love others can be placed on the vertical beam, the requirements to pour out and fill up can be placed on the horizontal beam, and the central circle can represent the goal of unity with God. Illustrating the Scriptures visually

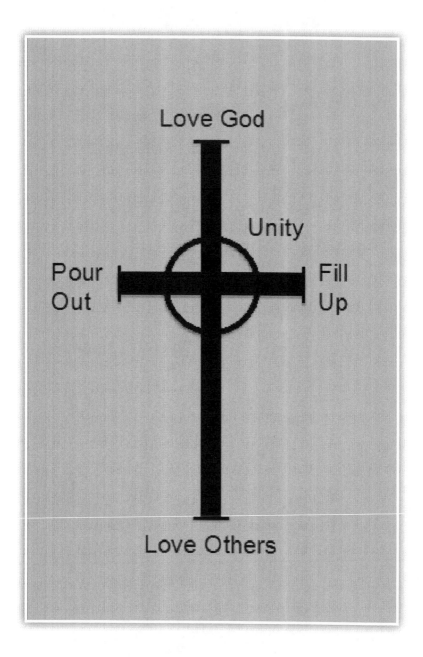

invites us to consider the points of intersection between the Scriptures – the four quadrants or spaces created where the lines cross. For example, the first quadrant, in the upper right corner, calls us to consider what it means to fill up through the love of God in a way that leads to unity with God and one another.

Placing the Scriptures into relationship with one another seems especially appropriate because that is exactly what Jesus did in the Greatest Commandment response recorded in Matthew. Jesus paired Scriptures from two sources, and placed them on equal footing by saying that one was like the other in Matthew 22:39. The statement of Jesus is not simple proof-texting or the parroting of the answer of a scholar - it is a statement full of authority. Jesus lived his life and fulfilled his ministry through loving God and loving people.

Seen as a whole, the model emphasizes the need for balance among the quadrants in moving toward the goal of unity with God. An over-emphasis on any single quadrant disrupts the balance of the cross. It is impossible to pour out before being filled, and Jesus' own explanation of the Greatest Commandment emphasizes the similarity between the love of God and the love of others. Within the model, one must live in each of the quadrants to grow closer to God.

Jesus models this balanced behavior. In Luke 7, Jesus withdraws to the mountain to spend time in prayer immediately before he preaches the Sermon on the Plain. In John 6, Jesus withdraws for time apart after the feeding of the five thousand. Seen through this lens of holistic behavior, Jesus moves from the love of God to the love of humanity seamlessly, living in his teaching that both are important and refusing to see his loving as a dualistic either/or proposition. Similarly, he recognizes the human limitations of his ability to pour himself out for others, and withdraws to fill himself with prayer and quiet. Jesus lived wholeness and balance, and did not allow himself to be drawn into legalistic thought.

Living in the wholeness of love and in the flow of giving and receiving resists legalism, which does not focus on love. The example Jesus sets in John 8 in his encounter with the religious hierarchy over the fate of a woman caught in adultery is an excellent example. The scribes and Pharisees appear quite willing to sacrifice the life of the woman in order to force Jesus into a politically compromising position. There is no love or compassion felt for the woman (where, by the way, was the man?), who was simply being used as a pawn in a game of personal power. Jesus refused to be trapped by the ploy, and looked through the legal issue to the fate of the woman and, surprisingly for anyone other than Jesus, to the fate of the accusers. Jesus helped the accusers to see their own sin, and either through shame or through enlightenment, the accusers withdrew. Only then did Jesus turn his attention to the woman, and instead of accusing her, he saw to her healing by moving her away from her sinful behavior. Jesus' sense of balance and wholeness kept him centered on the issue of love, and moved him beyond the simple and obvious legalistic answer to the real issue of the situation.

1 Peter 2:9 reminds us that all Christians are called by their baptism into ministry to the glory of God. From that statement, we infer that living in the tension between the Greatest Commandment and the "Hymn of Kenosis" requires people to live in that way individually and to help

others to live that way as well. Upon reflection, that idea makes perfect sense: In order to pour out, someone must be filled up, and vice versa. If our "pouring out" in order to love God involves leading worship, it is possible that another person will be "filled up" by experiencing the worship service. That concept emphasizes the importance of Christian community, by which God uses the gifts and graces of each individual to the glory of God and the benefit of others. Some individuals are set apart by God to provide servant leadership in this process, which is the role of ordained clergy. Some of the means of loving God and loving others, and of filling up and pouring out, require particular training, gifts, and graces, which is the role that those people fill.

Ministry in this light assumes a vitality and a continuous movement among the quadrants, and that failure to do so results in the stagnation we witness in the church today. Many people find that the focus, programs, and culture of the traditional church are no longer relevant in their lives. One can argue that this disconnection is caused by the failure to appropriately address all of the quadrants of Christian life and that it is the role of the minister to mindfully teach the importance of moving among the quadrants.

A holistic Christian life models this behavior by being centered on the love of God and humanity through a flow of giving and receiving with the goal of living into a unity of love with God and others that echoes God's love for us.

Food For Thought

How does your view of a holistic Christian life fit with the one described in this chapter?

Discuss the *Simple Harmony* model and how it might work in your life.

Are there other Scriptures you would use in defining a balanced Christian life? Why?

SIX

Worship

The upper right quadrant of the cross model represents actions that fill and strengthen a person that are related to loving God. These activities fall broadly under the category of Worship, but in addition to the public and private worship of God, they include prayer, receiving the sacrament of the Lord's Supper, and spending time in the reading and interpretation of Scripture. This quadrant includes activities through which God's grace typically flows to people, including those activities that are often referred to as "means of grace." The means of grace are the outward signs, words and actions that God has designated to be the

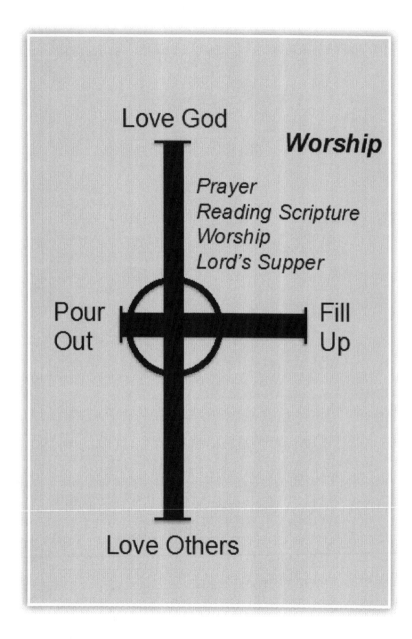

Love God

Worship

Prayer
Reading Scripture
Worship
Lord's Supper

Pour
Out

Fill
Up

Love Others

ordinary channels by which God conveys grace to people. They are actions and activities to be implemented in the course of daily life through which God frequently and routinely gives grace to people.

It seems at times that many Christians in the Western world believe worship services describe the entire role of the church, and perceive worship as one hour on Sunday morning to be included in the weekly routine to placate God. In the quest to move beyond these perceptions of the traditional roles of church into a more missional space, however, one cannot ignore the importance of preaching, worship, and the sacraments in filling people up to serve God and others. The key is recalling that the church is a body of people, not a building or a place. In his wonderful book *Not Every Spirit: a Dogmatics of Christian Disbelief* (Clark International, 2009), Christopher Morse provides insight in his comparison of the "union" of God with humanity through the incarnation of Christ and the "communion" of God and the church, as the "union" makes the restoration of the Greatest Commandment possible and the "communion" is a result of that restoration. A community of believers in communion with God would include both people in the process of salvation and people testifying to the process of salvation. In both cases, the church acts as a center of education and respite when people can gain refuge and recover reason. The church can be seen as a group of people who consciously self-identify in that role and who are a body of God's faithful people within which the Word is preached and the sacraments are administered. The church enables worship that in turn enables the individual and collective growth of the body of believers, and expands the number of people exposed to the Gospel. Each individual church is a part of the larger body of Christ that upholds the central tenets of Christian belief and acts on behalf of Christ in the world. God acts through the church in all of the Persons of the Trinity, but the church is most often associated with work of the Holy Spirit to teach, enlighten, and sustain humanity and the world. The church itself is a means of grace and is involved in the performance of many of the means of grace. It is important to note that the means of grace are not the exclusive domain of the church, and that means of grace can and do occur outside of the context of the church.

Worship fills us through the power of the Holy Spirit. Singing together, praying together, and engaging the preaching of the Word can all provide opportunities to connect with the Spirit. It is important to note that these activities are some of the common or routine ways that the Spirit connects with us, and that actual connection will change from time to time and from person to person. That observation supports the use of a variety of forms of worship and openness to what constitutes a valid form of worship.

Using the example of music, many churches have struggled with a perception that songs outside of the hymnal are not appropriate for use in worship. This attitude is based either in a clinging to orthodoxy and the attendant power and control issues that accompany it or, more generously, to the fact that many people feel a sense of comfort and connection to that music. Understanding music in worship as a means of grace through which people connect with the Holy Spirit to be spiritually filled encourages us to taste a variety of music, anticipating that something different might touch us or that something different might connect with someone else in a way that it does not for us. From that perspective, being critical of a person's musical offering in worship is offensive to God and to the person who has offered that act of worship. Music is our gift to God, not a means of entertaining ourselves. Similar arguments can be made for styles of preaching or forms of prayer.

The Lord's Supper also plays a critical part in the life of the church and believer. In his sermon "The Duty of Constant Communion," John Wesley emphasizes the importance of partaking in the sacrament as often as possible in obedience to the command of God and because it is of great spiritual benefit to the believer. He explains that the sacrament is a "continual remembrance" of the death of Christ and that the elements are "outward signs" of the inward grace of Christ. The Lord's Supper is spiritual sustenance - a way to feed our souls - as it touches us both spiritually and physically.

The Lord's Supper is a sacrament initiated and ordained by Jesus Christ in the first Christian community, the circle of his followers. The ritual of the sharing of simple foods is a sharing of the real presence of Christ among those present in a manner that reminds us of the suffering and death of Christ that brought about our redemption, and that reinforces the bonds of Christian community. The Lord's Supper touches Christians and Christian communities in a variety of ways.

Praying together has been a central aspect of Christian community as long as there have been Christians. In Romans 12, the Apostle Paul provides instruction to a young Christian community in living a life transformed by Christ. In verse 12, he teaches, "Be happy in your hope, stand your ground when you're in trouble, and devote yourselves to prayer." (CEB) Prayer in community is an action by which Christians communally and individually place themselves before God, offering praise, seeking guidance, and simply being in communion with God. One can imagine prayer in community as an embodiment of Jesus' prayer in the Unity Prayer. A community of believers, praying together, is connected to God and to one another.

It is not unusual for congregations and individuals to "get stuck" in a quadrant, to focus on it to the exclusion of the other quadrants. This results in an imbalance in living out the anchor Scriptures, which slows our motion toward deeper connection with God. For example, getting stuck in the Worship quadrant implies a disproportionate focus on the love of God over the love of others, and an imbalanced preference for filling up rather than pouring out. As we consider the characteristics of each quadrant, it is helpful to think about what "getting stuck" in that quadrant might look like.

Getting stuck in the Worship quadrant shares many characteristics with the sin of gluttony. A glutton is one who consumes excessively, often to the detriment of others. A worship glutton is one who focuses exclusively on their personal experience in worship, insisting that the setting, liturgy, music, and preaching be precisely as they like it because that is what fills them. The consumer mentality can be a significant component of worship gluttony, evidenced in the trend to shop for worship experiences as one shops for designer shoes. People can experience gluttony in Bible studies, in prayer groups and solitary prayer, and in church worship experiences. The worship glutton is concerned about their own experience and their own salvation without any intention to pour out what they have gained. Balanced worship sees the empowerment and inspiration of worship as a part of a larger experience that includes the sharing of the love and energy that flows from God in worship. We fill up in order to be empowered to pour out, not to become spiritually lethargic!

Food For Thought

Through which means of grace do you feel closest to God?

Does worship have to be in a particular format in order to fill you up? Why?

Is the Lord's Supper meaningful to you? Why?

SEVEN

Sharing

The upper left quadrant of the cross model represents kenotic acts related to loving God, remembering that kenosis is the act of pouring oneself out. It include actions related to making it possible for others to encounter the ordinary means of grace, such as preaching, leading worship, and teaching Bible studies and spiritual formation. This quadrant also includes the actions of witness and testimony, the sharing of the stories of God's action in life with the intent of participating in the spiritual growth of another. Together, the activities in this quadrant fall into the category of sharing.

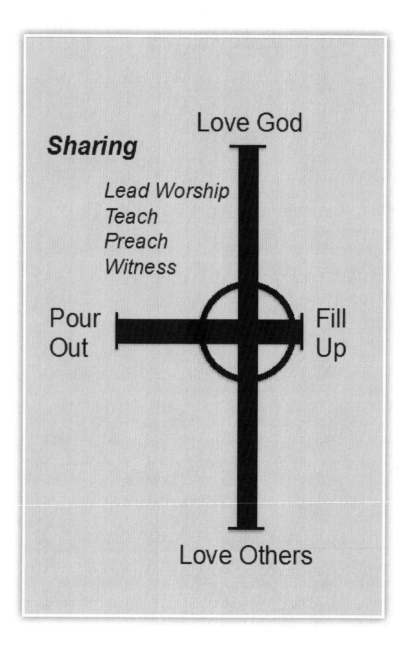

Notice the symmetry between the two upper quadrants. If listening to preaching is a way to be filled, then the act of preaching is a way of pouring out. If singing is a way to be filled, then teaching singing, leading singing, and researching singing are all acts of kenosis. The cyclical relationship between filling up and pouring out in this context takes on a deeper level of meaning when we return to the Unity Prayer as the explanation of why we do these things. We fill up and we pour out in order to grow closer to God and others ourselves, and to help others to grow closer to God and those around them.

The United Methodist Church states as its mission "to make disciples of Jesus Christ for the transformation of the world" and many other denominations place a similarly strong emphasis on sharing the Gospel. The concept of making disciples can be illuminated by considering the Great Commission found in Matthew 28:19-20 in relationship with the Greatest Commandment. If the Greatest Commandment defines *what* is to be done, and the Hymn of Kenosis defines *how* it is to be done, then the Great Commission defines *who* is to do it. People are to be made disciples through baptism and teaching so that they might live in the way that Jesus taught. Being a disciple is not, therefore, an end unto itself, but rather is an intermediate step of being drawn into a deeper relationship with God through the Greatest Commandment. Conversely, evangelism in this light is seen as a complete way of life revealed by Jesus Christ and empowered by the Holy Spirit, dedicated to loving God without restraint and loving others in ways that nurture, nourish, and equip them into the body of Christ. The objective of "making disciples" is to bring people into the cycle of living within the Greatest Commandment.

That is also an intermediate step, because of the goal of the transformation of the world. By making disciples, the church works with the Holy Spirit to bring individuals into a balanced relationship with God, and there is an cumulative effect brought about by bringing many. In *The New Conspirators: Creating the Future One Mustard Seed at a Time* (IVP Books, 2008), Tom Sine comments on the paradoxical nature of Jesus' teaching - that by focusing on God and on others instead of oneself, we "discover the good life that God has for us." The entire premise of Sine's book is that God has "chosen to change the world through the lowly, ordinary and insignificant." Sine envisions this occurring both inside and outside of the traditional "church" structure, freed from the constraints of dogma and polity.

Sine's insight relating kenosis to individual spiritual development turns conventional wisdom on its head. For many, the relationship with God is self-focused, concerned with personal salvation and the development of rules that keep others from bothering us or taking our material possessions. If pouring out one's talents and resources with the objective of loving becomes the focus of Christian activity, and a vital and growing personal relationship with God is the consequence rather than the sole objective, Christian behavior becomes radically different. The observation that God works through the lowly rather than the mighty becomes obvious simply because there are so many more of the lowly, and they are much less vested in maintaining the status quo because they have a much smaller stake in it!

Consider the example of a healthy hive of honeybees. Each individual in the hive is less focused on its personal well-being and is more focused on doing its individual task that brings health to the hive. Some bees gather nectar, some bees build combs and process the nectar into honey, some protect the hive, and some nurture the brood. The bees have a positive impact on the world around them by pollenating the plants that they visit. Their activities are focused on protecting and nurturing their queen.

Now imagine the example of that hive of honeybees, exchanging Christian people intentionally living through the love of God and each other under the direction of a loving and powerful queen, the Holy Spirit. The kenotic behaviors of the individual Christians vary according to their gifts, but their outward looking orientation has a positive impact on the growth of their companions and on their own growth. The actions of the Christians have a positive impact on the world outside of the "hive" and people who come into contact with the "Queen" through the words and actions of the Christians are brought into the hive.

The image of a hive drives away a focus on personal power and hierarchy, and it emphasizes the incredible potential of kenotic behavior under the direction of the Holy Spirit to drive a revolution of love throughout creation. Each individual, working within their own gifts and graces, doing their small part of living through the love of God and others, creates with God a positive impact on the world. By connecting through love guided by the Holy Spirit, individuals become communities, communities become churches, churches become societies, and the kingdom of God grows, here and now.

Leading worship includes a broad range of activities involving both clergy and lay people. It includes both the planning and execution of worship, and it involves every aspect of worship from the decoration of the worship space to the preparation of the liturgy to the selection and performance of the music. Worship can take place in churches and in other shared spaces, indoors and outside, in formal settings or informal gatherings. Practically without exception, any form of worship requires a leader or facilitator to guide the communal activities. That leadership can be highly active or very passive, but it exists in almost every case. Musicians, ushers, childcare workers, space decorators, and audio/visual technicians all play a role in leading worship.

Teaching includes activities focused on helping others understand, appreciate, and develop their relationship with God. It includes sharing in formal classes and informal discussions in any number of formats ranging from Bible studies to back-porch chats. The emphasis is on sharing insight and information with others who may not yet have it to help them to grow closer to God. Teaching includes aspects of both loving God and loving others, as many of the specific activities do, but I have chosen to include it in this quadrant because of its relationship with the Worship quadrant – God is loved by our actions that focus on helping others to be filled through the love of God.

Preaching is a specialized form of teaching that has to do with interpreting and illuminating Scripture. It is undertaken by both clergy and laity, and differs from teaching in its focus on Scripture and on its intention to act as a conduit for the Holy Spirit to speak through the preacher. Preaching is one of the means by which the relevance and message of Scripture is translated into modern life.

Witnessing is a healthy expression of *evangelism,* a word that has unfortunately been twisted from its vital definition and purpose into a term fraught with negative connotations and political overtones. For the purpose of this book, evangelism is a complete way of life revealed by Jesus Christ and empowered by the Holy Spirit, dedicated to loving God without restraint and loving others in ways that nurture, nourish, and equip them into the body of Christ for the transformation of the world.

From that perspective, witness does not involve aggressive pamphlets, bullhorns, or formula prayers. Instead, it is an openness and willingness to share the ways that God acts in one's life with others through actions and words. It is positive action combined with a willingness to attribute those actions to the power of God in one's own life and with an invitation to learn more. Witness is not about intimidation, shame and accusation – it is an invitation to enter into the relationship with God and humanity Jesus prayed for in the Unity Prayer. It is a sharing from one who is walking down that path with God to one who is searching for that path to follow.

Getting stuck in the Sharing quadrant shares many of the characteristics of the sin of hubris, of gaining an exaggerated sense of self-importance. The Sharing quadrant incorporates many acts of leadership, and leadership almost by definition involves power in relationship to others. It is an easy step to allow our egos to run wild, building a leadership role into a seat of personal power, control, and influence. Most of us have seen pastors who will never relinquish the pulpit, choir leaders who reject non-traditional music, and Altar Guild chairs who will not move the communion table. Getting stuck in Sharing occurs when individual egos overpower the focus on the love of God, replacing it with love of self.

Food For Thought

List two things that you are currently doing that relate to loving God.

What would the bee hive image look like in your community?

Why is witness important?

EIGHT

Serving

The lower left quadrant of the cross represents kenotic acts related to loving others. These are the iconic "caring for others" charges related by Jesus to John the Baptist in Luke 7:22 and described as the criteria for separating the sheep from the goats in Matthew 25:31-46. Activities in this quadrant include feeding the poor, caring for the sick, visiting the prisoner, and freeing the oppressed. These actions are related to the more equitable distribution of resources, the easing of pain and suffering, and the administration of justice.

It is difficult to overstate the importance of caring for others in the earthly ministry of Jesus. In Luke 4, Jesus addresses the assembly in his hometown of Nazareth as he begins his ministry. He chooses to read from Isaiah 61 - the mission statement of the suffering servant - and sets forth what can be seen as a mission statement for his ministry. In the Scripture, he addresses good news to the poor, healing of the sick, freedom to the oppressed, and the coming of Jubilee, the year of the Lord's favor. That theme flows through the earthly ministry of Jesus from beginning to end. John 19 recounts Jesus arranging for the care of his mother while hanging on the cross, caring for the widow and the weak to the moment of his death.

In his sermon "On Zeal," John Wesley emphasizes works of mercy as a means of grace, meaning care of the sick and the needy, feeding the poor, visiting the imprisoned, and other similar actions that act to quell human suffering. Wesley argues that God prefers works of mercy to works of piety, and that in cases where both are not possible, works of mercy should be preferred. He describes a vector that moves from love of God to works of mercy to works of piety to the church as an example of their relative priority.

Protestant suspicion of "works" dates back to the Reformation itself. Martin Luther is said to have felt that the Book of James should be excluded from the canon because of his perception of its focus on works. Over time, some have come to view this dualism between faith and works as a false one, and embrace the words of James 2:14-26 as a description of a cause-and-effect relationship between faith and works rather than viewing them as polar alternatives in the path to salvation. From the perspective of the model, it is the desire to love God and others that vitalizes pouring out to others, not a desire to "earn" salvation.

This perspective is also consistent with Paul's description of the Fruit of the Spirit found in Galatians 5. Kindness and generosity flow from our life in the Spirit if we choose to let the Spirit guide our actions. Serving those in need is a natural outpouring of our relationship with God.

On their face, the examples listed in the Serving quadrant are self-explanatory, but it is important to move beyond the acts themselves to the systemic injustices they represent. For example, it is important to provide people who do not have food with something to eat, but it is also very important to think about why they do not have food and to do something about that. Thinking through the symptoms to the causes and then acting to address them is a critical aspect of this quadrant.

Many mission activities in churches address symptoms rather than causes. Mission activities that address symptoms – food drives, painting projects, yard care – are important because they can help those in the position of serving to better understand the issues that occur in the lives of those being served, but without a focus on having that heightened awareness move into addressing the causes of those issues, the mission activities bear little long-term benefit. Pouring out in love to others involves relationship creation, not just service. Bringing a grocery bag of food to the church so that a poor mother will have food for her kids is important, but knowing that poor mother well enough to help her find a job is more important.

Loving others in this way is hard. It is much easier to go on a weeklong trip to build a building, or to bring used clothes to the church, or to simply give money, and those are meaningful steps in starting a journey within this quadrant. We must not lose sight of the fact that as we grow closer to God, we will need to move beyond simple service into the harder space of resisting forces that oppress people.

There are important synergies between the two kenotic quadrants on the left side of the model. Pouring out can bring benefits to the entire human being, to both body and soul. Seeing that breaks through another false dichotomy, the distinction between body and soul. God created both as the totality of created humanity, and one cannot neglect one and nurture the other. The distinction between kenosis in the service and love of God and kenosis in the service and love of others is a soft one better viewed as a continuum than as opposites. God feels loved as we share and serve because we are living into the vocation that God created for us. Others feel loved as we care for them spiritually and physically. The author of James frames the question in James 2:15-16, wondering what good it is to bless the poor with words of comfort when they are cold and hungry. Following the example of Christ, kenosis feeds the body and soul, the physical and the spiritual, with the goal of moving closer to God and others.

Getting stuck in the Serving quadrant calls to mind the image of "being a martyr." The church has been blessed by the service of many martyrs of the church who gave their lives in the service of the Gospel, but the martyr of the food pantry who gives and gives out of a personal need to fix problems and gain recognition has also touched the church. The example of Jesus found in John 12:1-8 provides a significant teaching in this regard. Mary anoints the feet of Jesus with an expensive perfume, and Judas criticizes her saying that the perfume should have been sold and given to the poor. Jesus defends Mary's action by pointing out that, in this particular case, attending to the Messiah was more important than serving the poor. Jesus points out that serving the poor is a lifelong struggle and that the needs of the poor are large, and that at times it is important to step away from that need to address another. The "martyr" fails to recognize that the work of the Serving quadrant is done for the glory of God through the power of the Holy Spirit, and that loving others in this way involves serving alongside God rather than fixing the problem on God's behalf.

Food For Thought

How are you serving others?

What does spending time in service mean to you?

When you have served in the past, have you come into contact with the people who are being served? Have you had conversations with those you have served?

NINE

Humility in Community

The lower right quadrant is perhaps the least intuitive of the quadrants. It deals with allowing oneself to be restored through the acts of others. This quadrant addresses letting go of the false self - of suppressing the ego - and allowing oneself to be ministered to by others. There are two primary characteristics within this quadrant: humility and community. Humility addresses submission and suppression of the ego in recognition that God's grace is sufficient and that the assistance and contribution of others is necessary in our Christian development. Similarly, this quadrant involves the recognition of the importance of community

as it focuses on the restorative nature of engagement within the body of Christ. Actions within this quadrant include accepting generosity, receiving grace, being loved, and accepting forgiveness.

In *Falling Upward* (Jossey-Bass, 2011), an excellent book about the two phases of life, Richard Rohr defines the false self as "your role, title and personal image that is largely a creation of your own mind and achievements." The false self is a construct that we build to present to the world that reflects our own efforts at building security. It is the product of answering questions like, "Who will you travel through life with?" or, "How will you earn a living?" We have all heard people answer the question, "Tell us about yourself," with a long list of job titles, educational credentials and family statistics. Those are false self answers. Conversely, the true self is the person who God sees, the person at the core of being.

The false self strongly resists actions in this quadrant because they require humility. In this context, humility is the releasing of the sense of personal power, authority, or hierarchy one has with regard to another. Humility is closely related to vulnerability, and the false self resists anything that may bring pain, discomfort, or powerlessness. Consider how often people turn down well-meaning and truly needed offers of kindness or assistance because they are unwilling to seem vulnerable.

The reaction of Peter to Jesus' offer to wash his feet found in John 13 is a good example of this behavior. Peter is aghast that Jesus, his rabbi and master, would offer to wash his filthy feet, a task that Peter culturally perceived as demeaning and lowly. Because it violated Peter's sense of hierarchy and appropriateness, he refused to allow Jesus to serve him. Jesus had to explain himself and to cajole Peter in order to break through Peter's false self to continue with his teaching. Peter's false self kept him from being filled by the love and the wisdom of Jesus.

The reaction of Simon the Pharisee to the washing and anointing of the feet of Jesus by the village harlot found in Luke 7 is another example of this phenomenon. Simon could not comprehend how Jesus would allow the sinful woman to touch or serve him. Simon's false self saw that as a breach of boundaries, hierarchy, and piety. Jesus, seeing from his true self, saw the woman's gratitude for her forgiveness and her need to physically express her submission and humility by washing Jesus' feet in an intimate way. Jesus allowed himself to be served, empowering the woman's need to serve, and being filled himself by her devotion.

It is not coincidental that both of these illustrations involve feet. Feet are personal - they get smelly and dirty, and they are physically sensitive - and most people have reservations about exposing their imperfection and sensitivity to others. The feet are a wonderful metaphor for the true self, and exposing them to others for care and washing is what this quadrant is about.

A willingness to be vulnerable and to allow others to access the true self is a critical element in Christian community. In an environment where popular Christian culture often emphasizes the "personal relationship" between Christ and an individual, it is important to step back and consider the nature and importance of Christian community. Without undervaluing the importance of personal justification and individual sanctification, the concept of entering into relationship with others in a Christian context may flow from as fundamental an idea as the nature of God. Christians, with very few exceptions, embrace the doctrine of the Trinity, an understanding of God as three Persons of one substance – a God whose very nature is community. It can be argued that the very rationale for the creation of humanity was to become part of that community – to join into the circle of love that exists among the Persons of the Trinity.

Jesus reinforced this concept in the Greatest Commandment. The common statement that loving each other is a mandate of great importance forms a definitional footing for Christian community as a relationship in which Christians love one another as Jesus loved them. Matthew 18:20 affirms this concept in Jesus' declaration that whenever two or more gather in his name, he is present.

The Apostle Paul wrote extensively on the concept of Christian community, often using the metaphor of the body of Christ to describe the interrelationship of individual gifts and graces to the corporate whole and to emphasize the importance of being followers together. Paul's letters that we see as canonical are predominately addressed to groups of Christians in a particular city. The frequency of Paul's statements on community is sometimes not as apparent to the reader of English translations because the English language does not differentiate between the singular and plural forms of the word "you." For example, Paul's important statement on the sacredness of the body as a temple of the Holy Spirit found in 1 Corinthians 6:19 is often interpreted as a statement calling for individual holiness while it in fact uses the plural form of "your," implying that the community is responsible for maintaining this sacredness. The Scriptures converge to allow us to form a working definition of Christian community from them. A Christian community is a group of two or more Christians with a common frame of reference who share God's love.

That sharing of God's love requires vulnerability. We simply cannot maintain the walls of the false self and simultaneously allow the love and concern of others to nurture us.

The addition of the final quadrant allows us to consider synergies once again. They involve the giving and receiving of blessings and comforts of other people. They involve selflessness, generosity, and the willingness to act from the true self. The quadrants on the right side of the model have to do with grace. The upper right quadrant represents the ordinary means of grace through which God brings grace into our lives. The bottom right quadrant is a recognition that God works through humanity too, and that maintaining an attitude of humility in community allows the grace of God to flow through other people into our lives.

Getting stuck in the Humility in Community quadrant shares many characteristics with narcissism, an excessive interest in oneself. A narcissist can allow others to serve them to excess without regard to pouring out in return. A narcissist can also become overly focused on the benefits of a particular group, dwelling within a particular community, or with a particular group to excess. As when one is stuck in the Worship quadrant, getting stuck in the Humility in Community quadrant involves an unbalanced emphasis on self to the exclusion of others. When Maria in *The Sound of Music* sought to withdraw to the safety and security of her abbey when she found herself in love with Captain Von Trapp, she was in danger of getting stuck in the Humility in Community quadrant.

Food For Thought

Do you have a community that you can share and be vulnerable with?

Why would this be necessary?

Is humility still a quality that society values? Why is it important for Christians?

Is it possible to love God and others all by yourself?

TEN

Sharing the Model in a Church

The Book of Ecclesiastes reminds us that there is nothing new under the sun, All of the concepts and ideas included in this book have been considered before in various combinations and contexts. Yet, in thinking about the practical application of this model with friends and in a church, it seems appropriate to begin with education. The components of this construct are as old as Christianity itself, yet the framework of their interaction and the implications of their intersections might not be apparent without clear explanation. After establishing a firm basis for understanding and growth through education, the

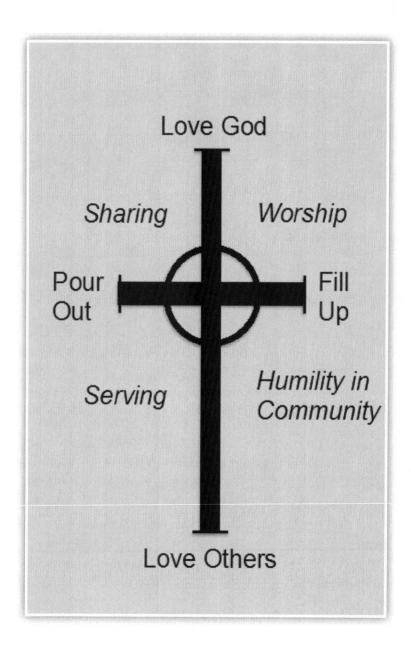

emphasis would shift to evangelism, which is intimately tied to the mission of the church. Laying out the evangelical implications would then usher in preaching and worship for illumination. This sequence establishes theory first, then ties it to the critical component of invitation, and finally settles it into Christian life.

Education - Daily Christian life can be guided through an understanding of Christ's teaching regarding the love of God and of others and of Christ's example of pouring out and filling up. While the anchor Scriptures are familiar scriptural teachings, seeing them as related and as shedding insight into one another is not typical. To vitalize daily life around this theological position will require a season of focused teaching at all levels. Individually, it will require prayer, reflection, and consideration, and within a community, time will be necessary to help the leadership and the congregation to grasp the key concepts and to begin to relate them to Christian teachings as a whole. Using this book and the Celtic cross graphic, it is possible to teach classes and to preach sermons that illuminate the key concepts of loving both God and humanity, of the need to fill up to be able to pour out, and of the holistic nature of this pattern of life - moving from quadrant to quadrant in a rhythm of life. The heart of the original educational push is very simple: to help people embrace the clear lesson and example of Christ as a means of living the Gospel.

Once the initial educational thrust is complete, the educational role of the minister-leader shifts to the role that Stevenson-Moessner describes in *Prelude to Practical Theology: Variations on Theory and Practice* (Abingdon Press, 2008) as the "conductor." It is not unusual for people, groups within a congregation, or even an entire congregation to get stuck in one quadrant, focusing exclusively on worship or too heavily on community service. The leader must continually remind the congregation about balance and touching all of the quadrants so that none of the aspects of the life Jesus taught and modeled for us are excluded. The diversity within the body of Christ almost guarantees that individuals will excel in some areas more than others, so it is critical that leaders continually teach the importance of all of the quadrants to remain balanced and whole.

Evangelism - Evangelism is at the heart of the mission of the church as an integral part of the transformation of the world. Implicit in living life in this manner is an invitation by example. Almost by definition, living in a balanced and holistic way that is centered in God will be attractive to many. Pouring out in the love of God includes teaching and preaching, and pouring out in love of others includes sharing the Gospel with those in need. This approach yields a very positive and attractive invitation to join into the process; the benefits to self and other are readily apparent. Living in this way also implicitly rejects coercive or fear-based evangelism; neither of those approaches are grounded in love. Bullhorns become irrelevant as people witness the benefit of the Gospel lived and proclaimed as simple truth rather than as dogmatic rules.

The social context of the specific church merits specific consideration in this regard. For example, my church home is situated in an ethnically and economically homogeneous area. Further, the predominate groups are the groups of power: white and wealthy. That fact, when combined with this model of Christian life, demands intentionality in evangelism at several levels. To borrow the phase that the teens in the church use, evangelism must take place both inside and outside of the "bubble."

Evangelism inside the "bubble" takes place as people live in the love of Christ and model rejection of the idols that plague our area. The model of living in balance is so foreign to the demands of sports, status, wealth, and power that are so rampant in our community that many will have difficulty understanding it. However, the rewards of idolatry are so fleeting and temporary that the model of life in Christ is very powerful. This evangelism really has very little to do with words - the noise of popular media is very difficult to be heard over anyway - and is much more about providing living proof in the community that the idols need not be worshipped.

Evangelism outside of the "bubble" will require deep humility and God's grace. From this perspective, evangelism must expand to include both inviting those who have not yet found Christ into God's Gospel *and* inviting those of different races and economic classes who love God to enter into Christian community with us. Growth in this form of Christian life will quickly reveal that without the love and input of Christians of all walks of life, the ability of our congregation to be a complete community of Christ will be diminished. Bringing other perspectives and points of view into the community will be critical spiritual nourishment for many - a filling up in the love of others that flows from unanticipated insights and the healing of old wounds. Pouring out to others in this context requires the rejection of patrimony and the patience to allow others see through old distrusts into the life lived in Christ. In this context, this is much less an evangelism of "doing for" than it is an evangelism of "being with."

As you have probably gleaned by this point, I am a United Methodist and tend to think about things from that perspective. For a wonderful discussion of evangelism and transformation of the church in this context, I encourage you to read *Longing for Spring: A New Vision for Wesleyan Community* (Cascade Books, 2010) written by my friend, mentor and ministry partner Dr. Elaine Heath together with her colleague Dr. Scott Kisker. Elaine and Scott have envisioned the recapture of holistic evangelism within the context of United Methodism, and their book is a way-point for those of other denominations seeking to do the same.

Preaching and Worship - The previous sections have included several observations that have obvious ramifications for preaching and worship, primarily in the areas of teaching and conducting. Looking at the bigger picture, worship should really be a microcosm of life lived in this manner; it should be vital, holistic, and true expression of love. Worship should fill up the worshippers with the love of God through prayer, song, preaching, and sacrament, and it should be an opportunity for all to express their love of God through service and adoration. These goals can be achieved in a variety of worship styles and through any number of worship elements.

There are two aspects of worship that could be especially helpful in this light. First, worship should include a significant commitment to giving thanks. Great intentionality should be focused on identifying the actions of God in the church, community, and congregation and on giving voice to naming them and thanking God for them. Being intentionally thankful helps people to see the places in their lives that God is acting through the people around them, which in turn helps them to be filled in the love of others and the love of God. Naming God's gifts and acts of grace and mercy in our lives personalizes them and makes them more tangible.

The other helpful aspect of worship is naming, acknowledging, and celebrating transformation in the world. The mission of the church is to make disciples for the transformation of the world. When transformations occur, both small and large, we need to sing praises and shout joyfully. When people find Christ, when new life begins, when addiction or oppression ends, when new love rises, or when suffering ends, the church needs to name it in worship and be filled in the joy of a step closer to the kingdom. We live in a society that thrives on feedback and on information. If we do not celebrate the steps forward, people will simply miss them in the noise of the world.

Worship in this context becomes much more holistic in that it is not simply about kneeling at the feet of God, but includes a real and meaningful celebration of God's action in the world and our part in it. Worship becomes a critical component in being filled for the service of God in the world.

Food For Thought

Would your church be a willing participant in this model?

How would you implement the three aspects of Education, Evangelism, and Preaching/Worship?

List three "first steps" you would take to begin this process.

Spend the next few minutes in prayer (either individually or as a group) lifting up particular needs and challenges, people to help, and divine inspiration for your congregation.

ELEVEN

A Concluding Thought

The model is not difficult. The anchor Scriptures are clear, and they resonate with the need that many of us feel to recapture the centrality of service and spirituality in our lives. The model is deeply Trinitarian as it seeks to engage us by the grace of God, through the redemptive power of Jesus Christ, and through the active agency of the Holy Spirit into a loving relationship with God and each other.

Living the life that the model reveals is a bit more difficult. The world bombards us with appeals to be self-centered and to place our individual needs above everything

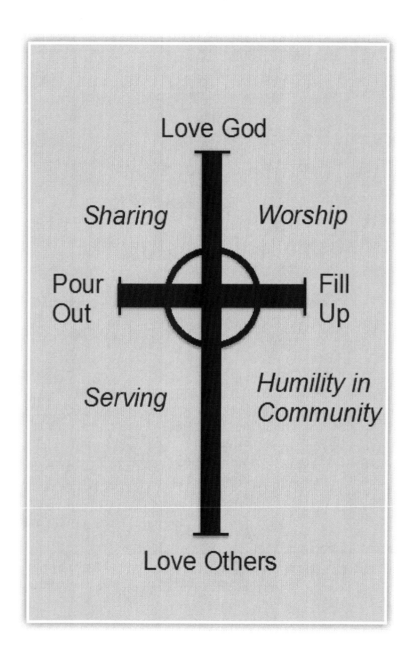

else. We measure ourselves against others in terms of wealth and power, and we seek personal security as a holy grail.

Yet the answer lies in the doing. If more and more of us chose to walk together with each other and with Jesus Christ on this path, God will work through the body of Christ that we can all be part of to make this world a better place. We are called to the kingdom here and now.

Sounds like a plan to me.